THE LEASE GUIDE

Commercial leases made easy for the entrepreneur.

How to save thousands on a commercial lease.

JASON DRAGON

Copyright © 2023 Jason Dragon.

ISBN: 979-8-86253339-2 Paperback
ISBN: 979-8-86254380-3 Hardcover

Printed by Amazon in the United States of America

First printing edition 2023

Independently Published by Jason Dragon:
9418 W Via Montoya Drive
Peoria, Arizona, 85383, USA

www.TheLeaseGuide.com

Letter to the reader:

Thanks for buying this book, it really means a lot to me. This book is full of useful info to protect you in the process of creating a commercial lease for your business. You bought this book because you felt that this knowledge would help you. I ask that you keep this book with you until you have finished it. I have kept it short so that you can read it in a day but it is full of the key things you need to learn to get a great lease.

The most important thing for me is that you learn and get the knowledge you need so that you and your business can win! So keep this book in your hand, or on your device and just keep top of mind until it is done. It could easily change your life.

Jason Dragon

Table of Contents:

Chapter 1

Introduction to Commercial Real Estate

I have been an entrepreneur my entire life. I was the Webelo in 4th grade who sold the most scout-o-rama tickets. I was the guy in high school who brought a bag of candy from the warehouse store to sell. By the time I was done with high school I was basically using the cash from my candy business to give high interest short term loans to other students. I knew I was destined to be an entrepreneur, so I went to college for small business management. I got to campus on the first day it opened and helped people set up computers, it was 1993 and back then they were not nearly as easy as they are today, and fewer people had them.

Once I was out of college, I ran a computer company for a short time from home but quickly found out that I needed a retail store to stock things, to have a place for people to go and most importantly to have employees. Back then a real business needed employees to work in the business while the founder and owner works on the business. Therefore, at the age of 22, I went out looking for my first commercial building to rent in. I knew enough about real estate to be dangerous, but I was at the start of this grand adventure.

I was going to sell computers, and one of the first few places I found had one of the premier locations to learn and buy CAD software and equipment. I quickly learned my first lesson in commercial real estate, the exclusive use clause. I knew about these, but I was shocked that the person running this company, who was twice my age, did not put one in their lease.

An exclusive use clause is a specific provision within a commercial lease that grants the tenant the sole privilege to conduct a particular activity. In the context of my computer company, this clause has been regularly utilized to ensure that I retain the exclusive right to sell computer hardware within the building. Any existing tenants engaging in the similar activities would naturally be exempted under a grandfather clause. However, I discovered an opportunity when I realized that a CAD business in the building had an exclusive use clause limited only to CAD software. Seizing this opportunity, I incorporated an exclusive use clause pertaining to computer hardware into my lease. This strategically allowed me to market computers that were superior in speed and quality compared to the existing options, and at a more competitive price. The implementation of this clause ensured my success at this new location, enabling me to sell 2-3 computers per week to their clientele. This not only covered all my operating expenses but also contributed to a consistent profit margin. A few years after I moved in the CAD company moved to a building they bought, but by then I was firmly established.

For the next 15 years I signed many leases experiencing a wide range of landlords. Some were with great landlords that treated me with kindness and flexibility. Others were strict and greedy. I even encountered one situation so problematic that I sold the entire location just to sever ties with that particular landlord. Through these experiences, I've generally, found that local landlords are much better than out of state ones and those are better than large corporate ones. The problem with the large ones is that the person who makes the decisions is just an employee and is not very flexible.

After the 2008-2010 market adjustments I quicky found that most landlords were much more corporate, much stricter, and much harder to work with. By this time my computer company mostly had business customers, and these business customers would tell me time and time how they had been destroyed by their lease, how they made mistakes at the start that made it hard for them to reach their dreams. I knew I could help them, but I needed a seat at the table, so I got my real estate license here in Arizona, with the focus of helping the entrepreneurs I knew stop making mistakes when it comes to commercial leases.

This was the beginning of my long adventure in commercial real estate. The problem is that I am only one guy and there are tons of entrepreneurs who need my help. I feel it is my obligation to help the entrepreneur community, so I have decided to write this book, to just put it all in writing. Once you know how to do simple things that make huge positive changes for a business you want to scream it to the world. That is why I am writing this.

We may never do business, we may never meet or talk, but I hope that the knowledge in this book will help you in your business and in your life. I hope that the new skills you will learn will allow you to help others whom you encounter.

My goal in this book is to help you quickly understand the basics of commercial real estate, and what you need to be a strong negotiator, so you do not fall into the traps of the landlords who are true professionals at this game. I want to do this with easy-to-use language and reduce the jargon to a minimum. I want you to win so I will give you all the tools you need so you are set up for success, I want to bring you so much value in this book that it makes a major impact on your business, setting you up to win.

This book explains the process of getting a commercial lease. This is a multistep process that we will cover in detail. First you select what you would like in a property, then you find the property. Then you make an offer on the property and once agreement is reached the landlord will write a lease. You then need to review the lease and make sure that everything you agreed on is in there and make sure that all the extra things are agreeable also. Once it is ok you sign it and launch your business. This book will explain each of these steps in detail. The goal is that you will know enough about commercial real estate that you can ask the right questions and get a good result for your business.

This book is meant to be written in, underlines, and highlighted. Use it as a workbook as part of your process.

Chapter 2

Huge Differences

The power of negotiations.

The power of negotiation is the difference between getting a great deal and getting a deal that could cause your business to go out of business. There are huge differences in the leases that one business may have, even if they are right next door to each other.

When someone goes to buy an office building, or the local corner strip mall you find a building that you are interested in and contact the selling party, and you want to know information about the property and the profitability of it. The first thing they usually do is ask you to sign a non-disclosure statement. They do this because they are about to share with you their finances and the rental agreements of all the tenants in the building.

Usually this comes in the form of an abstract, or spreadsheet where it will list every tenant, how much they pay per month, any exclusive uses, or other terms, when they have any future increases, if they have any renewal terms and when their lease ends. Sometimes it will show their payment history, and if they have a personal guarantee from the owner or not.

The shocking and striking part of this is you quickly realize that these deals are all over the place. One business may be paying $40 per square foot per year and the one right next to them is paying $10. One may have a 1-year lease, and another has a 15-year lease. But you quickly realize that, even with the same landlord, that there are huge differences. Most commercial real estate is priced on a PSF basis, price per square foot so it is easy to see these massive differences quickly and easily at a glance.

There are a few things that explain this difference, how full the building was when the lease was signed, how the economy was doing when the lease was signed, TI (Tenant Improvement) money given to the tenant, free rent given to the tenant and a few other things. However, many times, the differences are too large to explain away with such things, you quickly learn that it all comes down to how well the tenant negotiated when they were getting their unit.

Unless the landlord is a huge corporation we are usually dealing with emotional humans, who may be eager to make a deal today, and if your deal comes across their desk today you may just get a great deal. Other days they may not be flexible at all, they may have a price in their head, and they are unwilling to move.

There is a great number of landlords who seem to flock together, they listen to trends, and they often don't think about how local their projects are. They hear the national economy is weak and they look at a good business willing to sign a 10 year deal today, but at a much lower price than the going rate, they have fear of it going empty so they jump on it. They take that deal because in commercial real estate is common for unit in a property to be vacant for years and years, especially during a down cycle. As I write this it is 2023, and there is a lot of fear in the commercial real estate market. Landlords don't know how long it will be until they can fill their buildings. Some landlords have decided they want to put people in right now, so they get something during this time.

There are also huge differences in the management of these properties. I know of two strip malls near my home that are across the street from each other. One is owned by a local landlord, well-kept and is almost full. The other is bigger and for at least a decade has only had a pizza place and a karate place in it. The other 25 or so units in this building have been empty for years and years. The location is great and there is a booming college right across the other street, but the owners of this building are doing nothing to market the property or get it full. There is not even a number to call if you are interested in renting there. I got excited when I saw that it was being sold to a fund a few years ago, I thought they would do what the community needed and fix up this building and put nice businesses in there, but instead they carved off the hard corner of the lot to build a gas station. (A hard corner is the part of the lot that touches the intersection.) Nothing happened with the building, but if an entrepreneur wanted cheap rent and did not need to be in a busy building, they could find out who owns this building and make an offer of a lifetime to rent from them.

If negotiation skills are so important, how do you get there fast. First you will learn in this book the small hinges that swing the big doors. You will learn the strategies and tools you need to save thousands of dollars on your next commercial lease. But second you can simply hire an expert, someone who has this knowledge, someone who has these tools in their war chest, someone who will represent you in negotiating the commercial lease. The best part is that in most every case, your new landlord will pay this person for you, they will cost you nothing. Of course, I am talking about engaging with a commercial real estate agent to represent you. A good agent will educate you about the process, they will knowledgeable about the local market but most of all they will be a bulldog negotiating on your behalf to make sure you have the best deal you can get for your business.

The worst thing you could ever do is to call the number on the building. That number is either going to lead to the owner, or much more likely their agent. Their real estate agent, by law, has to put the interests of the landlord first, in every case they will be against you and in favor of them.

This person is a professional, he does this for a living and probably has done it hundreds of times, they know every place where they can extract more money out of you for their client, the landlord. They will tell you that this is the best they can do, and they will seem like someone you can trust but don't tell them your secrets. Sometimes the agent will offer to give you limited representation, meaning they will help you out a bit more, but they will still disclose that the landlord is their primary client. In these cases, you will still not be totally represented but it may be a bit better.

The huge problem is that going unrepresented can easily cost your business thousands of dollars over the life of the lease. The even bigger problem is that over 65% of entrepreneurs, signing their first lease, go unrepresented. This is a tragic and totally avoidable mistake that puts their business at a disadvantage from day one.

The Power of Representation.

When you are represented, a good agent will help you find the best property that will meet your needs and budget. Because they are not tied to one landlord they give you the power of walking away, and finding a different property, a landlord rep will almost never suggest this. They may tell you about properties that are off market or coming soon. They may have insights into the local market that they will share with you. Having someone in your corner in this process one of the major keys to success in finding the right property and also negotiating the best deal you can get.

To be totally covered you need someone who will represent you and, by law, have your best interest at heart. How do you find such a person? Well, you could just call around, maybe ask your favorite residential Realtor® who they would suggest. You could also call the phone number on one of the building you are not interested in seeing if the person representing that landlord would represent you to find a building for yourself. Many commercial agents will help people find other properties, just make it clear you are looking for them to help you find a property and that you already ruled out the one they represent the landlord on or else they may keep pushing you towards that one.

Because you are reading this book you also have access to my network of awesome commercial agents. Simply go to TheLeaseGuide.com and we will connect you with a local awesome commercial real estate agent. We are part of the Coldwell Banker network which is one of the largest networks of agents in the world. If you fill out the form on TheLeaseGuide.com with your information and what you are looking for our team will find you the perfect agent near you that can specifically help you with your local commercial real estate needs, and who is also trained in the principles that are laid out in this book. With someone like that on your side your success rate goes up astronomically.

If you are going to go unrepresented then it is even MORE important that you read the rest of this book, it will give you the basic education that you need to stay away from the biggest pitfalls that people find themselves in when negotiating a commercial lease.

Real Estate Commissions:

Currently commercial real estate agents are paid by the landlord for their services. The landlord offers a total amount of commission, it usually is an amount equal to some percent of the total lease value, or it could be an amount equal to a specific duration of rent paid, or it could be a flat amount. If the agent, hired by the landlord, brings the tenant they get the full commission, but if the tenant has an agent working for them, it is much less work for the landlord's agent and typically the commission is split. Because of this agents will work for you for free, or at a very low cost, because they know they will be paid by the landlord when a deal is signed.

There is a concept called precuring cause. This refers to the determining act or effort that successfully acquires a customer or transaction, basically they are the cause that resulted in the client precuring the property. So if you found a property by driving by and calling the agent on the sign and that agent told you about the property then that agent has precuring cause. They will receive the full commission from the landlord. If you want your agent to help you with the transaction, you will likely need to compensate them because they will only be able to get a commission from the landlord if the landlords agent is nice and generous.

On the other hand, if you saw the sign, and then you gave your agent the address, and they called the agent on your behalf they would now be the precuring cause, and they would receive a share in the commission, allowing you to usually pay nothing and still have top notch representation. So if you want to be represented and you want to save money, keep this in mind. Don't be in such a hurry and let your agent work for you. It would be a shame to have someone show you property after property and guide you though the entire process, just to do it all for free because you could not wait a few minutes and you decided to call a listing agent.

Internet listings:

Most agents will list the properties from the landlords that they represent online using a multitude of different websites. Loopnet, CoStar, CommercialSearch and Crexi are some of the biggest websites where you can find out about commercial real estate available in your local area. Different websites are more or less popular in different areas, in my area Loopnet is by far the most popular one.

These websites can be good for getting information and starting out your search, however they have a few big problems. The first problem is that they don't share complete information here, you need to call the landlords agent to get that information, and as soon as you do then that agent has precuring cause. A better idea is to send the address to your agent and let them get the information.

The next major problem is that there is no incentive for listing agents to remove leased units from these websites. I have had clients send me lists of 20 or more different units they are interested in and after a bit of research I find that only 2 are still available. They like to leave these up because it is a great way to get entrepreneurs to call them, where they could say, "Sorry that unit just recently rented, but I can show you a few others around town that I have listings on."

In my city I have found that for each type of property there are only a handful of companies that list most of the properties. For example, if you want a small warehouse for a business in the west side of Phoenix you can just look at CityWide, Cutler, or NAI. The nice thing is that each of the companies has their own website, where the listings are kept much more up to date than on the major sites. I have the websites for 20 such companies bookmarked, and for most of them I have people at each company that know me and are saved in my phone.

Pocket Listings:

As someone looking for commercial space you also need to be aware of pocket listings. A pocket listing is a listing that has not been shared with the general public and usually not online.

This can be for many different reasons. Maybe the landlord is not ready to list the property yet but will be soon. Maybe the agent wants to have a little while to market it to his list of people so he can get the full commission. Maybe the agent wants the property to look as good as it can so they are cleaning it up so that they can take better photos. Maybe they are just too busy to get it listed right now but will do it soon.

The nice thing about pocket listings is that they are usually the ones the agent is currently in the process of listing, so they are top of mind for them, while at the same time being hidden to the rest of the world. This gives you and your agent a chance to make an offer on a property without much competition.

I have found that listing agents are much more willing to share information about pocket listings with other agents, mostly because these listings are not ready yet and a bit harder to sell, so they let the tenants agent do the heavy lifting.

Be aware that terminology sometimes varies from region to region. I will try to introduce you to many of these terms and also explain them in plain English.

Hiring an agent.

When you hire an agent be sure to find one that is knowledgeable about the area and property type that you are looking for. It is best to interview two or three of them to find out which one you click with the best. If you don't have at least two, then visit TheLeaseGuide.com and we will find you one or two from our network and connect you with them.

Activity Item:

Write down the names and phone numbers of at least two local agents who you know. Call them and see if they can represent you. Select the one you click with the best.

Chapter 3

The property

Finding the best property for your needs.

The property

Before we can do anything, we need a property. The first step is to really think about the property that you want to lease. There are many things to consider when selecting a property and we will cover them all. The include, type, location, class, amenities, buildout and more.

Type:

Now you need to decide what type of property you want to have. Just because you plan to open an office does not mean that an office building is the best for you, and the same goes for someone opening a retail store. Imagine what it will look like, is it an office, is it in a strip mall? Is it in a flex industrial space? What part of town will this property be in? Does your business need visibility? Is the property going to be near a major road or will you be better served by the lower cost of being out of the way a bit? I am going to assume that you followed my advice and have a good real estate agent on your side.

The four main types of commercial property are Office, Retail, Industrial/Flex and Specialty. Office is just what it sounds like, space to make an office. Retail can be anything from a strip mall, to a shopping mall or even a stand alone building. Industrial space has more room for storage and has a warehouse attached. Warehouse space usually does not have HVAC and is cheaper and not very finished. Industrial space that has a larger amount of retail or office space is often called flex. Flex space is often some of the best spaces for new businesses that don't need traffic from neighbors to make their business successful.

Specialty retail space is anything that is built out for one type of use. Often this is churches, automotive uses, restaurants and medical facilities. If you are opening a business with one of these types it is usually best to look for specialty space, because it will likely already have a buildout you need.

Why rent instead of owning? Everyone knows that it is a path to long term wealth to own your own home, but when you want to open a business, it is much different. When you are first starting your business, and moving from home-based to your first location money is almost always very tight and it is much harder to get approved for a commercial loan when you have no track record. That is not even the main reason to rent, for most businesses being in a busy shopping center or office building is much more important than owning would be for their success.

Being one of 30 businesses in a busy center will bring you customers and sales, it is automatic marketing, a way to instantly get your community to know who and where you are. Leasing is easier and quicker. Usually these strip malls will have a marques sign you can put your logo on, and they will have 100's or even 1000's of people visiting per day, with each one giving you a chance to make a sale.

Leasing has much less upfront costs. In many cases you can find a unit that is already built out, and you simply need the first month's rent and a deposit around the same size to move in. When you are starting out you won't be able to spend the millions needed to buy a whole shopping center. Owning real estate is not your core business and right now you need to focus your attention and money on your core business. Maybe after you are in business for a while you may be big enough to buy a building.

If your business does not need customers to physically visit your location, you can locate in a lower cost space. If you are a service business that needs storage space, then an industrial space will likely be the best space for you. You often need to be creative when it comes to property types. I have personally found some of the best success with my business renting spaces in low-cost warehouse space where I can get a huge building for a lower cost per square foot. I have others who own service businesses and instead of putting their office in an office building they decide to put it in a retail strip mall. You may also consider if two spaces would be best, it is common in industries like bathroom remodeling to have a showroom in a strip mall with mock-up and salespeople, and then to have a warehouse where you store all the material needed for jobs. You can usually widen your view a bit and get a little creative in your search.

Action Item:

Write down the type of property that would be perfect for your business:

Location and amenities:

There are many things to consider when you are selecting your building. The location, the traffic around the area, the ability to install visible signage where that traffic can see it. You also want it to be convenient for your customers and your employees. If you are opening a bin or thrift store you don't want to be in the high rent, high end area because that attracts the wrong demographic. You want to consider public transit in the area if many of your employees and clients use that. If you need access to shipping, you want to consider how hard it is for delivery trucks to visit your property. Do you need roll up doors or garage doors, if so how many, how wide do they need to be, how tall do they need to be? Do they need to be at ground level or do they need to above grade.

If you need 3 phase electricity, large amounts of water, high ceilings, a dock for a truck or large amounts of parking then be sure to put all of those in your list of must-have or nice-to-haves. How many bathrooms do you need? Do you need a full kitchen or just a small break room or nothing at all? How much storage space do you need in the back? It makes your agent's job much easier if you know what are the things that your new space must have and what other things you would really like to have.

Action Item:

Write down what location requirements you have for your business. Parking? Visibility? Signage?

Write down the Amenities that are important for your business.

Class:

There are three levels of building classifications. There is a bit of grey area here, and of course when a building is between two levels it is often marketed as the better one. These classifications apply to all different types of commercial properties:

- Class A buildings are almost new, in a highly attractive location, and are known for good maintenance.
- Class B are average buildings, about 15+ years old, with fewer amenities.
- Class C buildings are older than 30 years, and they may need a lot of improvement and repairs.

Of course it is usually nice to be a newer building, however newer buildings typically cost more and often they are not as well known as something that has been there for 20 years. When you are looking at class B and especially class C buildings more attention needs to be spent on the structural aspects of the building. Ask about the HVAC system, the electrical systems, the plumbing and even the fire systems. Also many older buildings may not be built out for the fastest internet speeds. It is always a good idea to ask the neighbors how fast their internet is.

Size:

You also need to consider the size of the unit and the features of the unit. Do you need hard floors or will carpet be fine? Do you need to be on the first floor, do you need to be close to an elevator? How big does the backroom need to be? Can your business fit in a 1500 square foot space for the next 5 years, or can you afford a 1500 space with your planned business plan, even if things go wrong. You don't want to get too much space because you are paying for something you don't need but almost as bad you don't want to get too little space that it is hard for your business to operate.

Action Item:

Write down the size your business needs now, and in three years. Think about how much office, retail, and storage space you need to make your dreams come true.

It is also a nice thing to know what other properties that a landlord owns.

Landlords will almost always break your lease early and move into a larger space that they own. If that landlord happens to own 20 buildings in the area it will give you a much larger choice when you grow.

There is also a concept called Build-to-suit. This is usually raw land where the landowner will build a building custom for your business, and then you will sign a long lease to cover rent and paying back the landlord his build costs. Other times a landlord will be building a huge building, where multiple tenants will be moving in and they will start preleasing space before the building is even built, this is a great way to expand your business into a new and up and coming area, but it is not great for making your business now, this process can take years, and if an anchor tenant backs out it may never happen at all.

Buildout.

We have mentioned buildout a few times but I wanted to wrap it all up into a section. The buildout is the way the building sits right now. Most landlords don't make many or even any changes to a unit after a prior tenant leaves. This allows you to look for businesses that have the same or similar buildout to your business so that you can save a ton of money on making changes to the unit. If you are opening a barbershop, look for places that used to be a barbershop, and if you can't find one look for something wide open, with not too much storage. The less walls you need to add or remove the lower your tenant improvement cost will be.

Action Item:

What is the best current buildout for your needs?

Due Diligence:

In general there many things to consider when you are trying to find the building that is right for you. And you also don't want to get too attached to anyone building just in case you can't negotiate a deal you like. You always want to be aware what your other choices are. Because of how long the process is, if you are in a hurry you may want to start the process with multiple properties, and then weed out the ones that are not giving you the terms you like. In many ways it is like shopping for a car.

In general you need to do as much research on the property as you can. When I was building my most recent new flagship store for Emerald Computers, we really liked the building and we liked everything about it, the layout was almost perfect for what we needed so we were able to take it as is. But we found two major problems, first the AC system was not well designed. In fact they had an AC for the top floor and a separate one for the bottom floor, but the swap cooler air from the warehouse also blew into the front part of the build that had the AC, there was nothing to stop it, and in fact most of the ductwork was missing, the landlord then dropped the bombshell that they just installed the AC units the week prior and they just assumed the duct work was all set up. I put in my LOI that they had to fix the duct work and make it all function properly as a term of the lease. In most leases the landlord will guarantee mechanical functionality for a short period of time, usually a month. After that time then everything is the responsibility of the tenant. I found this out the hard way when I needed to use the shower for the first time a few months after moving in and realized that the drain would start backing up after about 5 gallons were put in it.

The second problem I had with this property was the internet, there was not high-speed internet available at all on this property. I knew that wireless technologies existed, so I simply asked the landlord, in the LOI, to give us permission to put a tower on the roof. I am a tech also so I knew I could bridge a connection from my home to the new store using point to point wireless technology because they were under a mile apart, and with a 30-foot tower on top of the 20 foot building along with a 10 foot tower on my home we could get point to point. This bridge connection worked great for many year, eventually internet was available at the building, and I moved out of that house, so we got direct internet on that building. Imagine if I did not do the research on the property to see if it had internet, and then I would not have asked in the LOI for permission for a tower, they landlord could have refused. The other option was to get internet ran from the local school, which the local ISP wanted $15,000, plus $500 a month for a speed slower than my bridge gave me. This could have been a very costly mistake.

When you are doing your Due Diligence, you also need to talk to the city or county government that the building in is and let them know about your proposed use. It would be really bad if you sign a lease for a property and your use is not allowed by the city. Unless you have a clause that lets you out of the lease in such a case, this could be a very costly mistake. This is more common with so called vice industries. Smoke shops, CBD, Vape, Tattoo, adult products, alcohol and other adult activities are just a few things were the government has some strict limitations. You may want to open a stirp club, but you did not know that 900 feet away there is a daycare, it does not matter that they are open only during the day and you only at night, the city may have a rule saying you need to be 1000 feet away. It is not your landlord's responsibility to know if your use will be allowed by the city or not. A good agent should know these things and could be a great help to you if you are trying to open such a business.

Use restrictions can sneak up on a lot of businesses. Maybe you sell pesticides and maybe your city says you need to be 500 feet from the nearest home. Maybe you make fireworks and need to be within 50 feet of a fire hydrant. It is almost impossible to know every case, that is why having a few good conversations with your government permit office will go a long way to figuring things out.

Subletting:

Subletting is when one company signs a lease, but they want someone to take over all or part of the space. When a lease is signed the landlord needs to be paid that amount each month, exactly as agreed. If the company does not pay there are many things a landlord can do to get the money they are entitled to. So an easy way for someone with a failing or shrinking business is to find someone else to pay the lease. Because these leases could have been signed many years ago they often are at lower lease rates, and can be a great deal.

Subletting usually happens one of three ways. First a company will sell the business and transfer the lease to the new entity, technically this is still usually a sublet. Next the company will just find a new tenant to take over the space, they make a new agreement with the landlord and start paying the rent. Last is when a company has more space then they need so they can divide out some of their space and rent it out to another company. I know of one near me where they leased 25000 sq feet, but now only need 15000 so they built a wall and are looking for someone to take the 10000 sq foot area.

Sublets are usually listed by the same company that usually represents the landlord, though for bigger companies I have seen them hire a different company to represent them.

Chapter 4

The offer.

Asking for what you need.

Once you have found a property you want to make an offer on, the next step is to write a letter of intent (aka LOI). This letter says that you intend to lease this property and it outlines your terms. If you have an agent, they will write this for you. If you don't, this is the step in the process where you are at the biggest disadvantage, because they will usually write it for you. This is the part where you want to put in many of your magic terms, which we will talk about in the next chapter. Remember to ask for all the terms that are important to you, remember the old adage, you have not because you ask not.

Things that are commonly in the LOI are as follows:

- The Property location
- The amount and type of the lease
- The use of the tenant
- The timing of the lease, when it will start, when it will end and if there are price increases or renewal options.
- The rights you are asking for, like exclusive use right, or first right of refusal.
- A short introduction about you, your company, its history, financials and what it does.
- The TI's and the timing of delivery and possession.
- Any free or discount rents.
- Parking.
- Who is representing who.
- If there is a personal guarantee
- There is usually a part about how the whole letter of intent is non-binding.

To define a few things. A Personal guarantee is where the landlord of has the right to go after the personal property of the person who signs the lease, and sometimes a separate personal guarantee form. So if your business goes out of business and you still have 40 payments of $2000 left to pay then you owe them $80,000 personally, and they have the right get a judgement to collect it. I have seen people lose their home because they signed a personal guarantee, so don't do it unless you have a good plan to make the business succeed. You will almost never find a landlord who will give a small business owner a lease without a personal guarantee.

Traditionally most leases have a "bump" or yearly increase. In the past it has usually been 3% per year, mostly to keep up with inflation, recently inflation has been a bit higher so 4% or even 5% per year is not unheard of.

Lease types:

There are 3 main lease types and one modification. Usually, a landlord wants to have the same type of lease for the entire building and their systems are set up to run a specific type, so in most cases this is something that is hard to negotiate on unless you are leasing the entire building.

Gross Lease: The first type is the most common for office buildings, and it is called a gross lease. It is the simplest, it basically says that you will pay $2000 a month, and that is what you pay, in Arizona and almost no other place there is also a city sales tax on that amount. But that it is it, the landlord covers all the costs for property taxes, for common area, for most maintenance, for keeping the bathrooms set up and clean, for cleaning the building, for the insurance on the building and sometimes even to have someone clean your office. In most, but not all, cases the Gross lease will also include the electricity.

Modified Gross Lease: The next type is similar to the gross lease and is often used on industrial properties, it is called an industrial gross lease or a modified gross lease. It is much like the normal gross lease except cleaning of your area is not included, and usually you pay for water, trash, electricity and often some repairs.

Net Lease: The last lease type is the most common for shopping centers and is sometimes used on warehouses and offices, and that is the Net Lease, NNN Lease or

Absolute NNN Lease. This is for the owner who wants to pay nothing or very little, they just want to collect rent and have the tenants pay for his insurance, his property taxes, and all common costs like trash and even the repaving of the parking lot and landscaping.

The Absolute version means that the tenant is also responsible for all repairs, if that AC stops working, or the roof is blown off the tenant or their insurance will be paying for that. When you pay for building expenses it is divided up based on the percent of the leasable square footage you lease. So, if it is a 60k square foot building with 50k of leasable space, and 10k of common areas, and you rent 5,000 square feet of the building you would owe 10% of the landlords, insurance, property tax, utilities, and all other expenses each month.

Percentage Lease: There is another term you need to be aware of, it is the Percentage lease, which in addition to whatever else you are paying you also have to pay the landlord a percentage of your gross sales. The percentage is usually only taken after a tenant brings in a certain number of sales. I personally have had a few landlords ask for this, but I was always able to get it removed. In some markets it is popular and in other markets it is almost unheard of. This can be added to any other least type but is most common for a mall. Often it is to cover a marketing budget, so they get everyone to chip in 5% of their gross sales to pay for the marketing.

One Bite

In most cases you have one bite at the apple. If you forget to ask for something in the LOI it is very hard to walk it back and ask for it later unless they reject the LOI, then you can ask as part of the negotiations. For this reason, I usually will not send the LOI until the next day, there has almost never been a time where I did not think of a few items I forgot.

When I write a LOI I usually ask for at least a few things that I would like to have but that I don't care about too much. This gives me something to let them have a win on. If I don't care about assigned parking but I care a lot that they pay for the weekly trash pickup I may "trade" the parking for the trash pick-up, letting each of us have a win. Next, I will ask for things that I am fairly sure they will reject.

One trick that the leasing agent will sometimes do is to send you back an LOI that they wrote, leaving a few of your terms off, and asking you to sign it. If something is left out that you really wanted, then this is the time to stand up and ask for it to be put back in.

The LOI is non-binding, so it is ok to play here while you throw things at them that you want, and they throw things at you that you want. Non-binding means that there is no agreement here, and nothing you say here is permanent or enforceable. This is where you need a good aggressive agent on your side.

Survivorship

In almost all cases the lease goes on no matter if the parties to the lease change. I have had a few times where the landlord sells the property during the lease, don't worry your lease is still intact, and the new owner must do exactly what is on the lease.

There are cases where the lease says that a new owner can give you notice to cancel the lease if they choose to do so. I have only seen this done once. It was a strip mall that was dead. An event center opened in the anchor suite of the strip mall. They had so many events and brought so many people to the property that the property filled up with businesses that were flourishing. The landlord decided to sell the building, but unfortunately for the event center they had a clause in their lease that if the new owner of the building wanted their space, they could cancel the lease with 90 days written notice, and that is exactly what they did, giving the event center a cancellation notice. It turns out the new owner was already in the event space industry and opened an event center in the same space, with a new name the month after the old one left. There was nothing that the owner of the event space could do other than find a new place and move everything there.

I have also seen leases survive the death of the person who signed the lease. Usually a person will sign a lease on behalf of a business, and the business entity will survive the person. There are many leases that have a clause where if the person who signed the personal guarantee dies then a new personal guarantee must be provided and if not they have the right, but not the obligation, to cancel the lease. When it comes to such things the clauses in the lease will have the final say. These clauses should be thought about.

Much more often is when someone sells their business. The lease can handle this a few different ways. First it can be a new corporate owner. This is where a different corporation will be running the business going forward, when this happens there is usually a lease assignment. Most landlords will charge a fee to basically change the name on the lease and have the new owner sign, often this fee is crazy expensive in the realm of $2000 or even $3000, other times it is a much fairer $500 or so. Of course you can negotiate when you write the lease if you think this may happen. In most cases the former owner will stay on as a backup personal guarantee even when they require the new owner to be the primary personal guarantee. If you are selling your business, you should probably put a clause in the sale agreement that if they default on the lease that the business automatically goes back to you.

At other times you may sell the whole company or maybe even just the majority ownership stake. In some leases it says that if the majority ownership of a corporation changes that the new majority owner must also provide a personal guarantee. Sometimes an assignment will also be done and carry the assignment fee.

In almost every case the landlord can change with no fees or issues to the tenant. In a case where the landlord changes, they will usually have the tenant fill out an estopple certificate. This is just a document that lays out the terms of the lease and lets the tenant sign showing the new buyer that the information he is given from the seller is correct.

Chapter 5

Magic Terms

Know what to ask for.

There are a quite a few terms that you will almost never see in a LOI, or a lease written by the landlord's agents. These terms are almost like magic the give the tenant power. They are  small hinges that carry and move the largest doors. The catch is that you or your agent needs to ask for these things. These terms, tips and tactics are things you can ask for that will save you money, make things smoother and generally make your life in this lease a lot better. This chapter will be a list of these terms, what they do, and how to use them. As you read this chapter be sure to circle the title of the terms that you want to have in your LOI or lease, and be sure to tell your agent about them.

As-Is

One of my favorite terms is the As-Is term. In many cases a building will need to be fixed up to make it ready for the tenant, this is called Tenant Improvement (TI) work. TI work is a huge headache for the landlord for many reasons. The tenant will often have a specific way that they want the property to be built and it is too much work and effort to go through the property management, and the landlord to get that done. The landlord is often remote and if they do the TI work, they will need to have someone manage it, they will need to find the contractors and maybe do bids, they also do not like to have an open-ended expense. The easy solution for the landlord and often for the tenant is to just take the unit as it is right now. Sometimes this may include items left by the previous tenant, or it may already be built very close to how you wanted it. Also, maybe you can just build it out in the future over time. A space that was already built out for a prior tenant is called a second-generation space. Often, I have found a building I wanted to be in that has many vacancies and I have the landlord representative open up multiple suites so that I can select the one that is closest to my need, and that is the suite I make the offer on.

In other cases the prior tenant had a very unique or outdated design that makes it hard for new tenants to imagine being in the space, so the landlord rips everything out, except for maybe the bathrooms and a break room or closet. This is called a shell or vanilla shell. Sometimes they want to paint the inside, and they often make it white, they call this a white shell or white box. Both of these shells will have lights and electrical, and the white shell usually has flooring such as carpet or tile and often a finished ceiling. A space with nothing in it, just concrete walls is called a gray shell, dark shell or cold shell. A shell makes it ready and much faster to have TI work done. The better the shell condition the cheaper and faster it will be to get the TI work done.   TI work almost never includes furniture, fixtures, and equipment, also called FFE this is at the cost of the tenant.

For taking the unit as is, you will get it much faster, you will be able to make it how you like it and the landlord will thank you by giving you money. A landlord usually budgets a set amount to the TI work. For example if you are signing a $2,000 lease for 60 months that deal is worth $120k to the landlord, and they usually know that they need to spend money to get it built out the way that the tenant needs.

At the end of the lease the landlord gets the improved space so really, they are investing in their own building. So often they are willing to give you their TI budget in the form of cash back when you are done with it, or other financial benefits. This cash back is usually called a TIA or Tenant Improvement Allowance.   If you are able to get the landlord to agree to give you a TIA for your project you can often do much of the work yourself, or hire people at a much lower cost than the landlord would, giving your company a nicer buildout for less money.

If a unit needs more work, they will give you more money. If a unit is almost ready to go they may give you nothing. You need to ask, or have your agent ask, probing questions to see what they think the TI work will be worth. Sometime the landlord's agent will directly tell you this amount, making it much easier to negotiate. Of course they don't always need to say the truth, it is all really a big game.

When I did my very first lease ever the unit, I was looking at was almost exactly what I wanted so I took it as is in exchange for 4 months of free rent. This was the runway my new business needed to launch. My most recent lease had an out-of-town owner, and I knew from conversations with them that it would take forever to get it done. I told them I would take it as-is and do the work myself and he would reimburse me up to 10k of what I spent within 10 days of my store being open to the public. It was a simple build, 1 new wall dividing the space, new flooring, new ceiling fans and then paint the whole thing. I got them to charge me $11,000 to do it and to have it done in 5 days. Two weeks after we signed the lease, we were open for business, the landlord was so shocked I got it all done so fast. If you can figure out how much it is worth for them to just be done with it and give you the property now you can save a ton of time and get them to pay you.

Free Rent.

Most people know to ask for free rent. In real estate jargon free rent is called rent abatement. Of course, if you are working with the landlord's agent, they will probably not bring it up. In most cases you can get a month of free  rent for each year the lease is long. So a 5-year lease can usually come with 5 months of free rent. Some landlords have been burnt by this, someone will open shop and take the free months of rent and then break the lease and disappear, and then they find out the person is broke, so the personal guarantee is worthless. Because of this they may give you 1 or 2 months right now and then some more a year from now.... they also may do 1 month free and 4 months of half price rent instead of giving you 3 months of no rent. Other times they may push the free rent to the end of the lease, or I had one lease where each February was free.

Anything goes here and being creative may get you more free rent. In any case you always want to ask for a bit more than is reasonable because you may get a bit more for doing so. In most cases when a landlord gives you a rent abatement, they will still want to earn the same amount of money as they would on the full lease, they do this by extending the lease term by the number of months you are given free rent. So if you sign a 60-month lease with 4 months free at the front, you will then pay for 60 months, making your lease a total of 64 months. The majority of landlords will ask for this and it is totally normal.

In most NNN leases the common area maintenance (Cam's) is not considered part of the rent, and even if you get rent abatement you may still have to pay for that. Common area maintenance includes many things, such as the electricity, trash and water in the common areas, the landscaping, common bathrooms, and also money being saved up for larger projects like repainting the building, repaving the parking lot and anything else that maintains the common areas. You may have to pay all, some or none of the triple next expenses or Cam's, Insurance and Taxes, during the free rent period depending on what you ask for and what they agree to. I have been successful on gross leases to almost always get this thrown in for free during the rent abatement period, and about 60% of the time on NNN leases.

HVAC Cap

As I have said in the past, I am in Arizona and it is hot here and it is very hard on AC units. Other places are cold and hard on heaters. In almost all leases other than gross ones, the maintenance and repair of HVAC units falls on the tenant. Because it is a $7,000 to $12,000 expense this is something that can destroy a business. I have seen businesses operate when their store was 95 degrees inside, I have seen businesses close up shop because they can't pay to fix the AC.

The solution I have for this is simple, you just put in the lease that the tenant is only responsible for the first $500 in repairs per year. I have almost never had a landlord push back on this, I tell them  that if it is working condition now it should be for the next few years and if they don't feel it is good enough to last 4 years then they should replace it now before I sign the lease. I have had one landlord who make it $500 per failure. So I paid $500, and they had some poor repair job done, and I had to pay $500 two more times before they actually put a new unit up there. For this reason the $500 per year is much better. Most agents, even ones that represent you, will likely miss this one, so be sure to bring it up with them.

In addition to just HVAC you may want to cover all mechanical issues, who pays what if a roll up door breaks, who pays for a water leak in the walls, who pays for tree that dies or a tree who's roots block the sewer from the building.

Anchor Loss

Back 20 years ago I put a store in a high traffic center, almost all the traffic came from a large national chain grocery

store. So I put in the lease that is the Anchor (What we call the largest store in a center) were to close for any reason that we could void our lease and move out. It really came in handy, that location was not doing well for us and then the grocery store closed. I had a letter to the landlord the next day with notice we would be closing also. It was the most abusive landlord I ever had and I was happy to be gone. If the center where you are going into has one large tenant remember to use this. You can also use this on office space but that is less common.

Holdover

A holdover is what happens if you have not extended the lease, but you also have not moved out. Landlords hate this when this happens because in most cases, without a lease, you can move out with just 30 or maybe 60 days' notice. They want stability for their centers, and they want to know who will be here for a long time. For this reason they put a holdover clause that usually says if the lease expires, and you are still there your new rent will now be 150% of the last months rent. During the lease negotiation, not during the LOI phase, I have asked for this be lowered to 105% or 110%. I have not had great luck with those numbers, but 115% and 120% usually do work. I ask for 110% they offer 120% we settle at 115%. This will usually not be used, if things are going bad you just leave at the end of the lease, and if things are going good you renew. The main place I have used this is when the landlord wants unreasonable renewal rates. I recently did a renewal of one space I rent, and the landlord wanted a 25% increase. The only other option would be to move out. Unfortunately that lease has a 200% holdover rate. I had another unit where the holdover was just 110% so we went month to month for 6 months before they gave us a lease we wanted to renew.

Commencement date at or after COO

In many cases landlords are not really in a hurry to get TI work done. In most leases your commencement date, the date you lease starts is set by the lease. So sometimes your buildout or TI's will take away all your free rent, taking away your runway to operate without rent for some time. I have another friend who has a restaurant, she was a perfectionist and so was her city inspector. It took almost 10 months for her to do the buildout and pass all inspections. The problem is that she only had 5 month of free rent, so she was paying expensive rent for 5 months without even being open for business. This mistake cost her over $20,000. If she had simply asked for the commencement date to start once she has the certificate of occupancy (COO, permission from the city for her to start operating her business) she could have saved so much money. Usually if you ask for this, they will do it instead of free rent. If you have a large buildout, or if you are doing anything where the health department needs to do inspections, I suggest asking for this. You can also put a clause in there that if the government will not give you a COO or business license that you have the right to be let go of the lease.

On a side note, any suite that has been occupied in the past had to have a COO when it was occupied. If you are not changing anything major in the suite you can usually just continue on the old COO. Things you can change include flooring, paint, lighting, fans, and even walls if the walls don't go all the way to the ceiling. I have used this a few times to make it easier and faster to move into a place.

Expanded use.

Think of everything you may be wanting to do in the future and try to get the use for your building as broad as you can. It is up to the tenant to define the use in the LOI, so be sure to define it broadly. Most landlords don't care that much.

I have often asked for an exclusive on the sale and repair of all computing devices. This lets me tell the landlord that he can't put in that cell phone repair store in this plaza because I have the exclusive use. Two years ago I was talking with the manager of the Gym I go to. He was upset because a smoothy placed opened next to him selling smoothies to his customers. He had a good agent represent him, so he had it in his lease that selling smoothies was his exclusive use. The problem is that the landlord forgot, and the smoothie place was already open for a few months. The gym only sold smoothies in bottles from a fridge, but he had this clause, and he could show harm. I told him to talk to the landlord, he ended up getting a lawyer involved and at the end the landlord gave him 25k in rent discounts to allow the smoothie shop to sell smoothies. It was the landlords mistake, so he paid the price. So for having this little and unexpected use in his lease he made more than all the smoothies he ever sold.

The goal here is to make a vague use clause both in what you plan to do and what is exclusive to you. Make it as vague as you they will let you get away with.

Measure Correctly.

I had one building where I paid rent for over 4 years, and then I decided to measure the building exactly, and found out that it was 80 square feet smaller than they had told me. I was paying rent based on the square feet. Unfortunately my lease said plus or minus 100 feet in my lease. I was able to fix the amount in the renewal but this mistake cost me a few thousand dollars over the life of the lease. This is a simple mistake you can avoid.

In the case of office buildings they will often add your percentage of common areas to your square foot space. So for example you are renting a space in a building with 2000 square feet of common area, your suite is 1000 square feet, and the entire building is 10,000 square feet. That mean that you occupy 10% of the rentable space, and you would also need to pay rent on 10% of the common area, so when you get your bill you will be paying rent on 1200 square feet, your 1000 and 200 of the common area. This ratio of 1200/1000 is 1.2 and that is called your load factor. Building with more common areas will have a higher load factor, you should ask your agent what the load factor is on the various properties you look at.

Company Vehicles

In many cases your company may have a company van or delivery vehicle in the future. In most leases it says that there is to be no overnight parking. You should ask for an exception for 1 or 2 vehicles right up front. I usually ask for this when I see the lease if they have that clause, I don't ask for this in the LOI. If you have a small space, and there is parking behind the building I may also ask for permission to place a storage unit up to

200 or 400 square feet in the parking area. You can buy a container in the future and use it for storage.

Another really awesome thing you can do with having permission to park a vehicle long term on the property, is that it lets you wrap that vehicle with your logo and message, allowing you to park it there to drum up business before you even get a sign or are open. Having this clause is a marketing trick also that will let your business start with a bang.

In addition to just vehicles you may want to ask about the ability to put a storage container on the property, this can be very useful at time.

Parking

The amount of parking you get is usually based on the space you are using. In many cases it is spaces per 1000 square feet. In most cases if there is ample parking or vacancies in the plaza this will never be enforced. But in other cases you may need to mention it in the LOI because you may need an exemption. In retail space there is usually a lot of open spaces because they want to have room for customers, usually 5+ spaces per square foot. In office space there is less because it is usually mostly workers, and in industrial spaces it can be under 2 spaces per 1000 sq feet. Some cities have less space so they give you less parking spaces.

A common example is a church that opens in an area that has lots of industrial space. Let's say the church uses a 8000 sqft space with a ratio of 1.5. That means they can only have 12 cars parked there, so they need an exception. So they could ask that on nights and weekends they will have no limit and during normal weekday business hours will be limited to the 12 spaces. Most landlord would have no problem with this as it would not interfere with other tenants, but such a thing must be asked for in the LOI. If you need an exception, simply ask for it in the LOI, if you don't they may not mind you going over parking requirement from time to time. I have been known for having large parties at my warehouses sometimes, usually for Christmas, these generate large amounts of cars.

In addition to parking totals you may also want to know about parking locations and if there is any assigned parking. This is much more common in office buildings. For example you may be given 4 assigned covered parking spots for your company, and then unlimited uncovered parking. In some cases you have to pay for the assigned parking spaces, they may even require that you pay for a few of them to even sign the lease. A typical rate in Arizona for assigned parking spaces is about $25 a month, but I have seen them in cities with a lack of parking be well over $500 a month. This is something to consider.

Late Payment Fees.

You never know what will happen, and sometimes you can't avoid being late on the rent. I have it in all my leases that as long as the payment is made on or before the 10th day of the month it will be counted as if it has been made on the 1st day. This has saved me a few times when cash flows were tight. It also made it easy for me to simply pay my rent on the 7th each month, because I have other bills due on the 1st. My landlords are used to getting my payments on the 7th now. Also, they sometimes have a crazy high late fee. I have had some success in making that much lower. A recent lease I did had a fee of $400 if 5 days late, we changed it to $100 after the 11th day. All you gotta do is ask.

First right of refusal

This is an important clause to remember if you want to expand. It also can be called the Right of Expansion. You can make this work a few different ways. It means that if, for example you are in suite 102 and suite 106 is vacant and larger, before they accept an LOI from a new person they have to give the right to refuse that suite first. It sets you up for moving from your current suite to a larger one. Sometimes it is only for adjacent ones where you may have the first right of refusal only on suite 101 and 103 when you are in 102, and you would still need to stay in 102, you would just expand. If you ever think your business will grow quickly this is important, giving you the chance to expand, usually on the same terms per sq foot as your current lease.

I buy my suits from a local shop that was always small and crowded. Next to it there was a small bakery. During covid the bakery went out of business, and the suit shop had a first right of refusal on adjacent shops. They quickly contacted the landlord and was able to expand their shop to be in both suites. They make their new store fresh and bright and have been much more successful for doing this.

Renewals

When you are creating the lease, you can ask for renewal options. This is a great way to get certainty on how much you will be paying for the long term. I recently did a 5 year lease that has 2 renewal options at 3 years each. These options locked in a annual rate increase of just 2.5%. That is awesome in a time where inflation is over 5%. This means that the business can be there for 11 years without a large increase.

In the past I have signed leases where the landlord would not give us a renewal option. They usually do this so that they can increase your rent much more at the renewal time or that they can have options on what to do, especially if they are selling the property soon. Landlords love to give the new buyers more options, they usually pay more for the property.

This has never turned out good for us. In one case the landlord went bankrupt, and a hedge fund bought out the building, and they were very aggressive about raising rates, they wanted to almost double my rent at the end of my 3.5-year lease. I was unwilling to do that so we had to move that location, at great cost, to a new location. But the new location was much better designed and larger so it turned out to be a great move. The only problem was at the new location they also did not want to give us a renewal option. After a 5.5-year lease there we renewed, paying a 15% price increase, but we were able to ask for a small list of improvements to the property.

That renewal was for only two year so when that was over they really squeezed us giving up almost no more improvements and taking on a 27% increase, there was little we could do as prices in the local area were up over 50%, if we just could had been more persistent at the start about renewal options this would have never happened. Because of the personal pain from this, I really focus on this when I am helping clients secure the future of their business.

Subletting

Be sure to at least ask for good terms in case you ever sell your company. If it costs $3000 to transfer the lease that will make your selling price go down by that same amount usually. Be sure to make it easy to sublet and low cost. Also try to get it in the lease that you can sell the company and as long as the company name is the same there is no need for a sublet and that the lease just continues with no assignment fee. Some landlord will give this to you with ease and others won't. I have never had a landlord not significantly reduce the assignment fee if we asked for it.

Option to Buy

This is a clause I wish I had on my main building. You can put a clause in the lease that says that the tenant has an option to buy the property before a specific date, and either for a specific price or a price generated based on a formula or from an appraisal. This is most common when the tenant is renting the entire space. Because this clause ties the landlord's hands, they are fairly hesitant to give this to a tenant, and often only if a higher price is paid for the rent or a fee is paid for the option up front.

Be Creative

There are many other things you can ask for in specific situations. Be creative, think of everything before you sign that lease, this is your one chance to get everything you want. They are eager to get you into your building and are willing to give away a lot to get you to do so. I have often gone a whole month going back and forth to get it all perfect. Once you sign it is all over.

Representation

The best way to make sure that this whole process works smoothly and that you have the best chance of getting everything that you want is to have your own commercial real estate agent representing you. When you make sure these magic clauses are in your lease, and you have someone who is reading over everything, helping you draft everything you will save tens of thousands of dollars during the life of the lease. There is hardly a deal in life where you can get more and pay less.

If you need help finding a good local agent, we would be honored to have you use a local agent that we have vetted and who understands all of these concepts. If you would like us to connect you with such an agent simple visit TheLeaseGuide.com and click the find an agent button.

Chapter 6

The Lease

The ruling document.

Remember that everything is negotiable. I was one in a shopping center that had an on-site security guard. They had a rule that every business must be open from 9am until 5pm on weekdays and 11 until 4pm on Saturday. You could be open more but not less. The guard would check a few times a day and if your business was ever closed for any reason, you would receive a $100 fine paid to the landlord each time. A few  businesses were paying this fine many times per month, usually for opening a few minutes late. But I quickly saw how this was a problem for a computer business that may need to do emergency on site jobs for customers, so I told them I would not sign a lease with this in it, and they did not even bat an eye, it was taken out of my lease. My neighbors, who all went through the landlord's agent, were told this was not negotiable.

In commercial real estate almost everything is negotiable. The lease is your final chance to negotiate, once you sign it you are done.

After the LOI is accepted the landlord will almost always draft the lease. When the landlord gives you their first lease, they will add a ton of things to the lease that were never talked about. Most landlords send this task out to a secretary, or someone who basically just takes the terms from the LOI and copies and pastes them into a standard lease they use for most everyone. It may have terms in there about warehouses when you are renting an office. Many times I have found that the landlord's agent has little idea what is in the lease, they just send it to you, and most tenants are so excited to get a lease they just sign it. BUT that is the worst thing to do. This is not like buying a home where the one who makes all the paperwork is the title company or the lender, this paperwork was made by the opposing party. They will often leave out things in the LOI that you really wanted and that the landlord already agreed to. They will often add things to the lease that are totally out of the blue. And often they won't even know it was done, they just did a copy and paste from something they found somewhere else. It may talk about common hallways in a building without any, or security guards when there are none.

So when I first get a lease, I start with a blank word document, and I go through the lease from front to back and write down everything that I want to have changed. There are 100's of crazy clauses that landlords like to add. I have seen things that are illegal, to other things where they want to take some of your rights away. Some examples, I am in Arizona where much of the population carries a gun, and the landlord was from Denver where guns are mostly taboo, so they had a whole paragraph about how no one can carry a gun and how I must kick out any employee or client if I find that they are carrying one. That simply won't work in

Arizona. In another case they wanted to have photos of all your employees, photos of their cars and their ID sent to them. This was hard when you have many stores and you rotate your employees between them. The landlord would not budge on this so we walked away.

Remember that you have no obligation to keep negotiating with them, and that you can walk away and start over any time before you sign the lease. The power to walk away is one of the largest negotiating powers that you have. You never want to get emotionally attached to one property.

Once you get your list of changes then I like to try to have an in-person meeting with someone representing the landlord, if that is not possible we do zoom or email. You go one by one on your list, trying to see why they are asking for things. They often will have a good reason for many things they are asking for, other times it is a mistake or something they don't care about at all and you can get it fixed with ease. If you don't ask for something to be fixed it won't be fixed, so ask away, I often have 30-40 things I want changed on the first draft.

Again you want to pick your battles, and you may want to start some battles that you intend to lose. You can ask for a list of changes to be made to the lease knowing that a few of them you don't care about at all. These are changes that you will let them win on, and maybe trade for a win you actually care about. For example you may not care about parking at all but you can ask for two assigned parking spots so that you can trade those away to get something else, like free garbage services, that you really want.

The other thing you need to be aware of is that sometimes, and it seems to happen fairly often, they agree to remove or change something in your lease, and when you get the final draft, it is back in there. I have fallen for this trick before. We had a lease where they wanted a personal guarantee. The landlord agreed to remove it and in the next few drafts of the lease it was not in there, then when we got the final draft, the one that actually counts, it was put back in. However, it was not in the other drafts, so I did not catch it, so now that lease has a personal guarantee.

There are a lot of things in most leases that are very standard, your agent should help you with that. They will require you to get insurance, they will require you don't abandon the building, they will ask you help them with estoppel certificates if they ever sell or refi the building. (Estoppel certificates are just a fancy way of writing a summary of your lease and having you sign it saying that it is correct and you are still in the building.) There will be sections on what happens if you don't pay, or if the building catches fire, and what happens if you sell your business to someone else. It will cover if you have a personal guarantee, how the renewal process should go, any rental increases or late fees and much more. Most of the lease is very standardized and that is why it is so easy for an experienced agent to spot crazy things.

Once the lease is signed it is the gospel that your entire experience with that property will be based on. It is a system, a set of rules about what they will do if this happens, what you must do to conform to the lease and how the lease ends or gets renewed at the end. Sometimes we may make mistakes but sometimes they make a huge mistake. I once had a lease where we were supposed to receive 6 months of free rent, but the landlord thought he would be funny and make it 12 months of half priced rent on a 6-year lease. I said fine, but he decided he would make the last 3 months of the lease 3 of the half-priced months.

Fast forward 5 years, we are here to negotiate the lease, and I sent an LOI saying that the new lease would be 5% over the amount due of the last month of the lease. They signed a two-year lease renewal with this clause in it, but because that last month was half priced, I got the new two year lease for half price. Some heads did roll at the company for that trick. But I am bulldog, this is a game to many of them and to me and I want to win. I want to get the best deal for my companies and for all of my clients. So many landlords are so abusive of their tenants, and they beat them up to no end. Other landlords are a dream to work with.

I have a friend of mine who opened a restaurant, it was a run-down building in a bad part of town, and this was before I met this friend, he signed a lease for the restaurant space, thinking that his restaurant will flourish, but it was late 2019 and before he even was finished building his restaurant out the world shutdown.

He was given no tenant improvement money from the landlord, he was only giving 3 months of free rent, but with all the permits and then Covid, he was paying rent for almost a year without his business being opened. By the time he called me about it he had lost over 100k, and to make matters worse it was an 8 year lease, the lease was priced almost double what restaurant space in the area was leasing for, most of the plumbing and the AC did not work correctly and is 100% his responsibility according to the lease he signed. To make it even worse he has a personal guarantee. So even if the company goes bankrupt or even if he sells the business and the rent is not paid they can make a judgement against him, and take everything he built up during his life. He is desperate, the restaurant has not had one profitable month in its history.

The last time I talked to him he was thinking about selling everything and moving back to his home country, the only way the landlord can't go after him. It is sad, this horrible lease, bad timing and a not thought-out business plan has ruined his life.

WARNING!

This is the final warning. Once you sign the lease you are on the hook for everything that it says, it will set your future, the future of your business in both good and bad ways. Be sure to take it slow, think about every part of it and make sure this is what you want to do. Be sure to have a plan B in case this goes south. The only way out of most leases if for you to provide someone, who is acceptable to the landlord, to take over the lease. It can be someone that will operate the same business that you are in but it also can often be someone with a totally new use, as long as the use is allowed. Remember that many tenants have exclusive uses and in a large complex you may find it hard to find an allowable use due to these restrictions. Keep at it because you are paying the rent until you find a replacement tenant or until the lease expires.

You will need a couple of things when you go to sign. Most landlords will require you to have insurance before you can sign the lease. There is a standard form for insurance called the Acord form. On this form your landlord will have specific terms that must be on there. Most landlords will require you to have at least a million dollars coverage for accidents and such, they will also usually require that they are listed as an additional insured party. Your agent will create this form and give it to you. When everyone on both sides has signed the lease it is now called a fully executed lease. Usually you will receive an email with a PDF file that has the fully executed lease, this will be the lease version that is gospel going forward, be sure to save this file in a safe place, and not just in your inbox.

Next most landlord will require a check to be given to them. For a newer startup this will often be a cashier's check. It is usually the first month of paid rent plus the deposit. A deposit is usually somewhere between 1 and 3 months' worth of rent, though 1.5 seems to be the most common for people with decent credit. Usually the "first month" part will be the first month where full rent is paid. You should be given this total in the lease well before signing.

Once you sign the lease you may be given the keys and access right away, in other situations it may take a few days. If your lease is not commencing right away it could be even longer. Talk to your agent and the landlord to get this timeline so you are not surprised.

Chapter 7

After Signing…
LAUNCH!

Making a smooth takeoff.

Now that you have a lease you have a strong lease that gives you and the landlord benefits you simply need to perform. You need to get to work and make sure your business is a success. Remember all of the things you signed. They are enforced by the contract and in the case of default by law.

You need to follow the letter of the lease. In many leases it says that you will not allow any contractor to put a lien on the building. Some contractors want to be able to put such a lien on the building, and I had to not take the lowest bit on a project I had because they wanted a lien, but I signed a lease with my landlord saying I would not do so. You want to never be late. I would rather not pay my houses mortgage than to be late to my landlord, luckily I have done neither.

Speed

Time is of the essence, this means that the main thing the lease is about is time. You are paying a cost for the time you are there, so make the most of it. Don't waste any days, build it out as fast as you can, press vendors into doing things faster. If it is costing you $200 a day be willing to pay $1000 to a vendor to get things done two weeks faster. Get your sign going so it can be up as soon as possible.

During Covid I signed a lease for a new store. It was a simple redesign, adding one wall, installing new ceiling fans, new flooring and repainting the whole place.   I found a home flipper guy who was between flips, hired him and the day I got my keys he was in there, ripping out the old floors, I picked out new LVP flooring from a local shop, he went and got it, we put in the wall, then pained, then installed the new flooring all by the 6th day after getting keys. While he was doing this I had packed up all the inventory I needed for the new store, and even bought all the starting furniture and had it in my truck. By the 8th day the contractor was all done, we unloaded the furniture and shelves, put the inventory on it, ready to go with pricing our inventory.

Here is the quick checklist we used for our retail store, of course if you are setting up an office or a warehouse it will have some differences. Please put an arrow in front of all the ones that are important to you. Our list:

- ✓ Design your space: draw the layout.
- ✓ Hire a contractor to do everything to build your store.

- ✓ Contact the government for the proper license and permits.
- ✓ Get the internet connected, install wires for network.
- ✓ Set up server and point of sale computer.
- ✓ Set up bank accounts.
- ✓ Set up a merchant account and get a credit card machine.
- ✓ Install and set up security cameras.
- ✓ Install a set up a security monitoring system.
- ✓ Obtain business insurance.
- ✓ Buy and build all the furniture needed.
- ✓ Set up shelves, slatwall and displays for inventory.
- ✓ Acquire inventory and stock and price the store.
- ✓ Get an Echo from Amazon for music.
- ✓ Set up printers and hours on door.
- ✓ Stock bathroom with supplies.
- ✓ Stock a breakroom, get fridge, microwave, and food/drinks.
- ✓ Buy office supplies, artwork, open sign, fire extinguishers.
- ✓ Set up website and google pages with new address
- ✓ Print new flyers and business cards with the new address

We just knocked out this list and by the end of Day 9 we were done, ready for business, took some videos, set it up on social media, set up our google maps, yelp, apple maps, and such and people were shopping at our store on day 10. The landlord said they never saw something like that. I got 5 month of free rent, and I wanted to be open as long as I could to use that runway to launch the business.

You may notice that I did not have a phone system on my list. I personally have found it best to just use cell phones in my business. We use a company called Nextiva to create an IVR system, you know where it asks you to press 1 for this and 2 for that. We then have messages that answer the most common questions but if they want to talk to us they have a button that will just ring our cell phones.

If you need computer hardware, that is the primary function of my main business, we would be happy to connect with you and give you a great deal on the computers you need to launch your business. Simply visit

EmeraldComputers.com for more information. We ship all over the US.

    When you start a new business a flood of people will call you to start various services, the biggest one to watch out for is the merchant services. Some of these companies are very aggressive because they make huge profits simply because they are charging you huge fees. Because they know you will probably find a better merchant service company quickly, they will often make you sign a long contract with them.

    I will give you a huge shortcut, we have tried many different merchant services companies and have found one that gives us an awesome deal. I have worked out with them that anyone who calls them and mentions my name will get the same deal I have, this will probably save you half the money you spend on merchant transactions, the company is AppStar, and I have a personal rep there named Tim LeBeau, simply call him at 858-427-0771 and mention Jason Dragon to get the same special deal that I use. This one step can easily save you $1000's.

Your Marketing

You don't just want to get your building set up quickly, you need to jump start your marketing. When you open a business, you are not just in the business of the thing you do. For your core business to be successful you also need to be in the marketing business, you need to figure out how to get people to be your customers and to build rabid fans. Only once you master marketing to attract prospects, and sales to turn prospects into customers can you actually do your real business.

If you don't already have a logo, get that done now. A quick way to get a decent logo is to use fiverr.com. Then come up with a marking tone and theme, what colors you will use, what fonts, what graphics. Think of mottos, slogans, and such that you can use in

your marketing. If you think about this early enough, you can build your colors and logos into the actual structure of your business. All of our stores have the color green on the walls, because we are

Emerald, we are the green computer company. So it is natural that it should all be painted green. At our main store we had a large tech room where we were installing tile flooring, so I figured, why not spell out the word Emerald with the tiles.

Entire books are written on the subject of marketing. Let me tell you about a few that have changed my business. *Scale* by Nicholas Trevillian. *Sell like crazy* by Sabri Suby. *Way of the Wolf* by Jordan Belfort. I have a curated list of books and tools I use for my business on Amazon, simply go to

https://www.amazon.com/shop/jasondragon or scan the QR code to access this list.

Before you even open you need printed materials. A business card and flyer at the bare minimum. Then you need to get these into the hands of other people.

Next you need to get your signage ordered. Almost everyone can have window signage, and in retail plazas you can have a large sign on your building. Get this started early because a sign takes a few months in most cases. You can even start getting the sign done before you move in so it starts letting customers know what is being built. For me signage has been a tricky thing. The landlord will have requirements, and so will the city or county that you are opening up your business in. The sign company will design a sign with the requirements in mind and then they need to get the landlord to agree that this design meets the requirements of the complex. Next they will submit it to the government and then if the government like it you will finally have permission to build the sign. A typical sign is well over $5000 once you pay for permits, design, building and install. It is important to know this well before you open your business. The other thing is that this process can easily and often take 6 months or more, so getting started on this and following up is key, it is too easy to get busy and forget the next step in this long process.

Tell everyone you meet about your new business, tell people online, tell people on social media, tell your friends, your family. Don't keep it a secret. You can even tell the local newspaper and the chamber of commerce.

Next you need to work on the online part of the business. A google maps page is going to be your best friend, it is probably going to be the main source of new customers for your business. Once you have that you need a Facebook page and maybe even a group. You will want Instagram, Yelp, Apple Maps, and YouTube to be started right away also. Then to start to build a following and build excitement for your new business post small videos or other content often and regularly on as many locations as you can. The more you post the more you will get noticed and the more the sites will spread your message. Visibility is the key to marketing and success. If you need help with any of the marketing aspects, I highly recommend dfypromtions.com. They will help you with the key points that will help you launch quickly.

Your neighbors

Be a good neighbor. Most leases have the right of quiet enjoyment, this means your neighbors have that right also, so you can't have loud noise or do things in the common areas that will affect them. If they are making noise that is disturbing your business be sure to tell your landlord right away. It is in your landlord best interest that you are profitable, and they will help you with that.

It goes much further than that. Your business will be next to these businesses for a very long time. Make friends with the other business owners, introduce yourself, tell them what you do, give them business cards, take their business cards. Send them dream customers and they will probably do the same for you. Work with them to build a community. Maybe create a Facebook group for the building and have all the owners be a part of it, there is so much you can do when you work together.

When we had our flagship store in a large commercial complex we got to the point where we did business with over 50% of the businesses in the complex. After a few years we needed more space and moved our main store out of that complex and now, over 8 years later, we still get business from that complex almost every month. The power of relationships is very strong and can be the leverage you need to start your business with a boom.

Your landlord

The last and one of the most important things is to remember that your relationship with the landlord is a business relationship that will last a long time and the key to any good relationship is to talk, lots of open communication will really help. Let them know if there are problems and keep them in the loop about any major changes with your business. A good landlord will want you to be successful.

In many cases you will work directly with your landlord, but in other cases, especially when the landlord owns a lot of property, you will be working with a property management company the landlord hired to work with you. In some cases the real estate company that represents the landlord in the sales process will also the property management and in other cases a different PM (Property manager) will be your direct contact. I have also had a few rare cases where the landlord wants to remain anonymous, and the building will be held in a corporation or trust where the property manager, or a law firm is in control of the property. In this case all communications go through the PM and in many cases, you will never know truly who your landlord is.

Almost every landlord or property management company uses an online portal to process payment. Many PMs don't even allow you to send in checks anymore, they only take payments on the portal. It is important to sign up for the portal early. In the portal you will see past, current, and planned transactions. You usually can find a copy of your lease and other important documents. By far the most common portal software is called Commercial Café. I currently have multiple PM's that use this portal and it makes it easy to pay my rents, I just go to one portal to pay rent for unrelated landlords, it is very convenient.

You also need to remember when your lease is going to expire and start the renewal process 6-9 months before that date. You want to have the ability to find a new place and move if the renewal is not going to happen for any reason, including if the landlord has unreasonable terms. If you are looking to move at the end of your lease, please remember this book, and be sure to check our website to see if there is an updated version.

Activity Item:
Gather all of the information for your new landlord and their property management company. Get the names and numbers of their handyman, the accounting person and your property manager. Save all of these numbers in your phone.

Activity Item 2:

Write down the steps that are most important to you, use this area to make a checklist of the steps you will take to open your business.

Conclusion

I wrote this book because I want you to win.

I want your business to be successful!

I want to help you with this process, let's connect online by going to.

TheLeaseGuide.com.

We will match you up with a local Commercial Agent that will help you on your journey. We will help you with questions and guide you through the process of finding your dream property and negotiating your best lease.

If you have questions about this process, we are here to help. To do this we offer a FREE 30-minute consultation for people who bought this book.

To book a meeting to talk more about your commercial real estate needs, go to:

TheLeaseGuide.com/30

To Join our Facebook Community go to:

www.facebook.com/groups/leaseguide/

Acknowledgements:

Special thanks to everyone who helped motivate me to write this book.

To my wife who put up with all the late nights. To my coach, Nicholas Trevillian, who gave me the motivation to just get started and do it.

For helping me edit this book:
- Matt Wolfe
- Ricardo Cortazar

Icons and clipart: www.flaticon.com

About the Author

Jason Dragon is the founder, and General Manager of Emerald Computers, one of the largest computer companies in Arizona. Jason also runs Arizona Computer Recycling and a marketing agency called DFY Promotions. He is also a Commercial Real estate agent with Coldwell Banker Realty in Tempe, Arizona. He is a proud husband and father of 3 young men. He is active in politics, his church and community. He has built his business for over a quarter of a century and has been a real estate agent for over a decade.

You can contact him through dragon@jasondragon.com.

Visit JasonDragon.com for more information and his main links.